Days, Months, and Seasons in Haitian-Creole

Berwick Augustin

EVOKE180 PUBLISHING | LAUDERHILL, FL

Copyright © 2022 by **Berwick Augustin**

All rights reserved. No part of this publication may be reproduced, distributed or transmitted in any form or by any means, without prior written permission.

Berwick Augustin/Evoke180 Publishing
Lauderhill, FL
www.evoke180.com

Publisher's Note: This is a work of fiction. Names, characters, places, and incidents are a product of the author's imagination. Locales and public names are sometimes used for atmospheric purposes. Any resemblance to actual people, living or dead, or to businesses, companies, events, institutions, or locales is completely coincidental.

All rights reserved. Except as permitted under the U.S. Copyright Act of 1976, no part of this publication may be reproduced, distributed, stored in a retrieval system, or transmitted in any form or by any means- electronic, mechanical, digital, photocopy, recording, or any other except for brief quotations in printed reviews, without the prior written permission of the publisher.

Printed in the United States of America

Translated by Evoke 180 LLC

Days, Months, and Seasons in Haitian-Creole/Berwick Augustin.
978-1-7377826-6-7 (Hard Cover)
978-1-7377826-5-0 (Paperback)
978-1-7377826-4-3 (Coloring Book)

Dedication

For my wife Gretchen and children, Nyah, Ayana, and Prince.

After faith and family, language is a fundamental tool to one's heritage.

Dedikas

Pou madanm mwen Gretchen ak timoun mwen yo, Nyah, Ayana, ak Prince.

Apre lafwa ak fanmi, lang se yon zouti fondamantal nan eritaj yon moun.

Contents

Days of The Week / Jou Nan Semèn Nan 1
    Sunday / Dimanch 2-3
    Monday / Lendi 4-5
    Tuesday / Madi 6-7
    Wednesday / Mèkredi 8-9
    Thursday / Jedi 10-11
    Friday / Vandredi 12-13
    Saturday / Samedi 14-15

Months of The year / Mwa Nan Ane a 16
    January / Janvye 17-18
    February / Fevriye 19-20
    March / Mas 21-22
    April / Avril 23-24
    May / Me 25-26
    June / Jen 27-28
    July / Jiyè 29-30
    August / Out 31-32
    September / Septanm 33-34
    October / Oktòb 35-36
    November / Novanm 37-38
    December / Desanm 39-40

The Seasons / Sezon Yo 41
    Winter / Livè 42-43
    Spring / Prentan 44-45
    Summer / Lete 46-47
    Fall / Lotòn 48-49

Days of The Week
Jou Nan Semèn Nan

SUNDAY

Sunday

Today is Sunday.
It is the first day
of the week.

DIMANCH

Dimanch

Jodi a se Dimanch.
Li se premye jou
nan semèn nan.

Monday

Today is Monday.
It is the second day of the week.
Yesterday was Sunday.

Lendi

Jodi a se Lendi.
Li se dezyèm jou nan semèn nan.
Yè te Dimanch.

TUESDAY

Tuesday

Today is Tuesday.
It is the third day of the week.
Yesterday was Monday.

MADI

Madi

Jodi a se Madi.
Li se twazyèm jou nan semèn nan.
Yè te Lendi.

WEDNESDAY

Wednesday

Today is Wednesday.
It is the fourth day of the week.
Yesterday was Tuesday.

MÈKREDI

Mèkredi

Jodi a se Mèkredi.
Li se katriyèm jou nan semèn nan.
Yè te Madi.

THURSDAY

Thursday

Today is Thursday.
It's the fifth day of the week.
Yesterday was Wednesday.

Jedi

Jedi

Jodi a se Jedi.
Li se senkyèm jou nan semèn nan.
Yè te Mèkredi.

FRIDAY

Friday

Today is Friday.
It's the sixth day of the week.
Yesterday was Thursday.

VANDREDI

Vandredi

Jodi a se Vandredi.
Li se sizyèm jou nan semèn nan.
Yè te Jedi.

SATURDAY

Saturday

Today is Saturday.
It's the seventh and
last day of the week.
Yesterday was Friday.
Tomorrow is Sunday.

SAMEDI

Samedi

Jodi a se Samedi.
Li se setyèm jou e
dènye jou nan semèn nan.
Yè te vandredi.
Demen se Dimanch.

Months of The year
Mwa Nan Ane a

JANUARY

January

January is the first month of the year.

JANVYE

Janvye
Janvye se premye mwa nan ane a.

FEBRUARY

February

February is the second month of the year.

FEVRIYE

Fevriye

Fevriye se dezyèm mwa nan ane a.

MARCH

March

March is the third month of the year.

MAS

Mas

Mas se twazyèm mwa nan ane a.

April

April is the fourth month of the year.

Avril

Avril

Avril se katriyèm mwa nan ane a.

MAY

May

May is the fifth month of the year.

Mɛ

Me

Me se senkyèm mwa nan ane a.

June

June is the sixth month of the year.

July

July

July is the seventh month of the year.

Jiyè

Jiyè

Jiyè se setyèm mwa nan ane a.

AUGUST

August

August is the eighth month of the year.

OUT

Out

Out se uityèm mwa nan ane a.

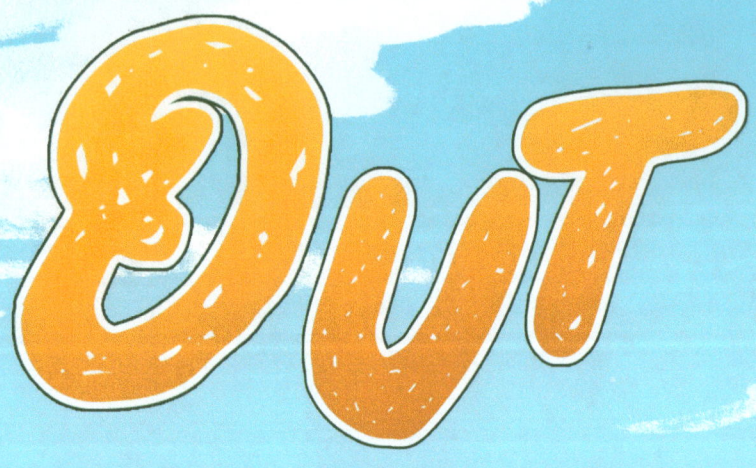

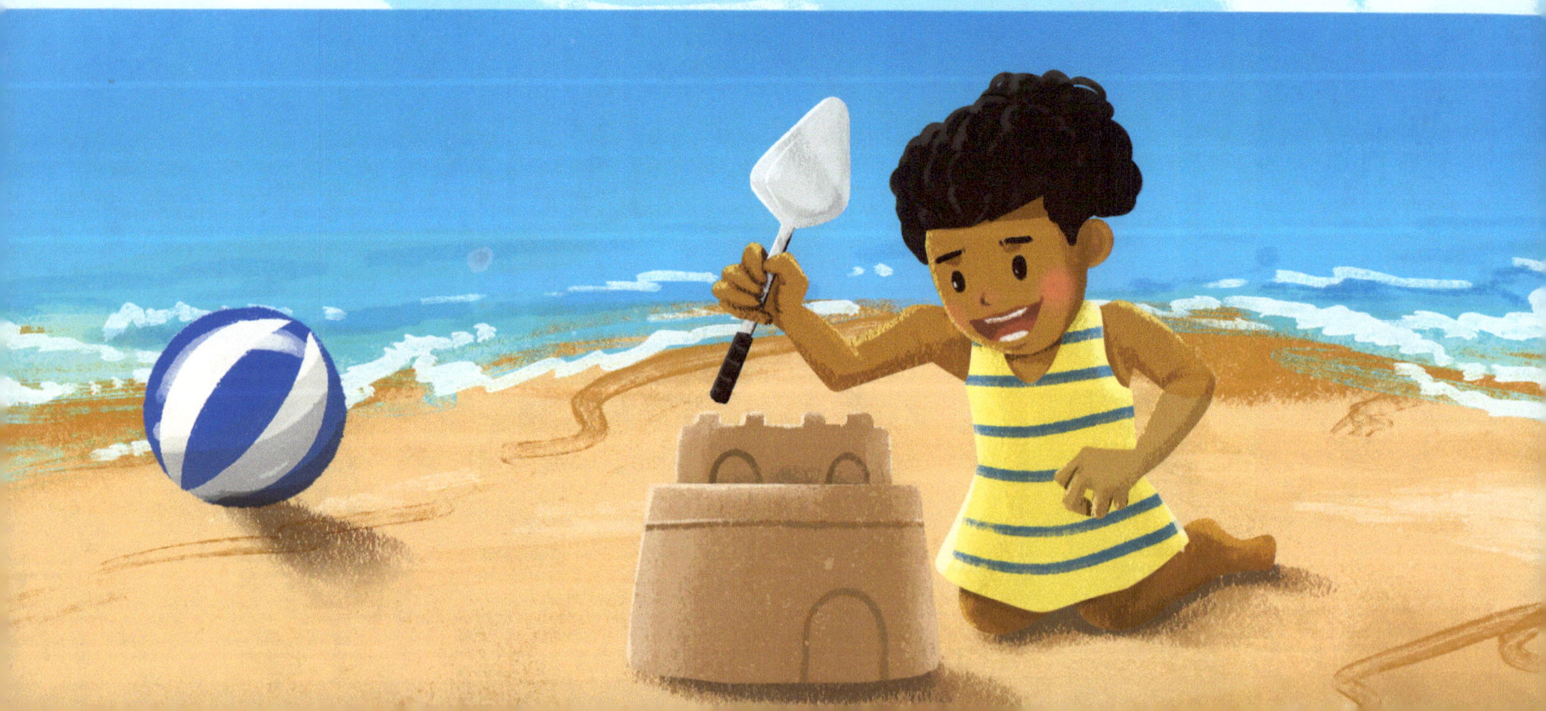

September

September

September is the ninth month of the year.

Septanm

Septanm

Septanm se nevyèm mwa nan ane a.

Oktòb

Oktòb se dizyèm mwa nan ane a.

November

November

November is the eleventh month of the year.

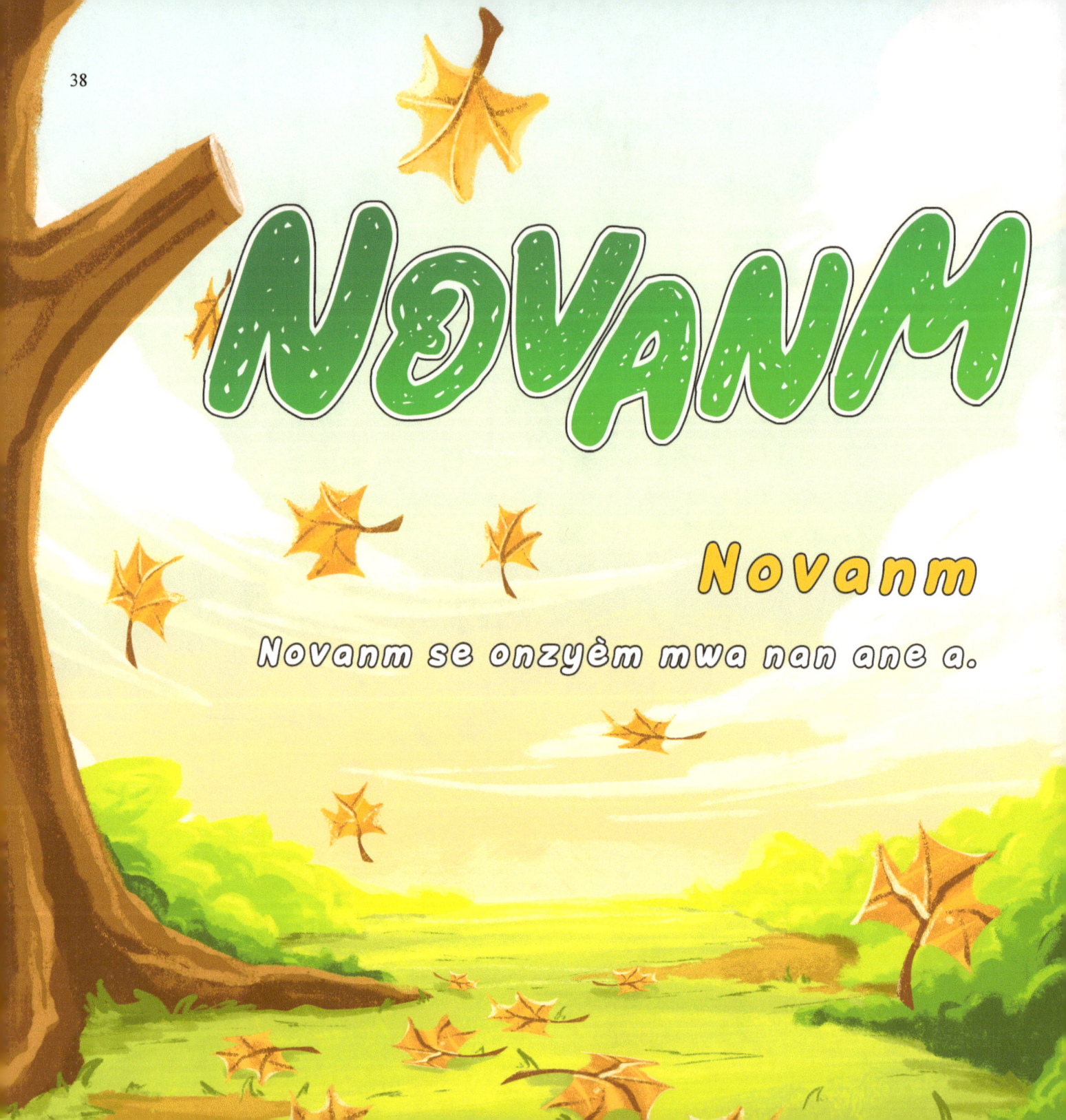

NOVANM

Novanm

Novanm se onzyèm mwa nan ane a.

December

December

December is the twelfth month of the year.

DESANM

Desanm

Desanm se douzyèm mwa nan ane a.

The Seasons
Sezon Yo

Winter

It's cold during winter.

Livè

Livè

Li fè frèt nan livè.

SPRING

Spring

Flowers bloom in spring.

PRENTAN

Prentan

Flè fleri nan prentan.

Fall

Fall has beautiful flowers.

Lotòn

Lotòn
Lotòn gen bèl flè.

ALSO BY BERWICK AUGUSTIN

1803-The Haitian Flag is an English/Creole bilingual story of two elementary aged siblings who are eager to participate in an annual Haitian Flag Day celebration at their school. They come to appreciate their culture after their parents teach them about the history, meaning, and symbolism of the Haitian flag. Children's Historical Fiction 978-099918221-5

1803-Black Freedom is the second book in a series of bilingual stories that promote Haiti's culture and history. The plot is centered around Pouchon, a middle school student of Haitian descent, who is trying out for his school's soccer team. His short stature makes him believe it's impossible to compete and make the team against bigger and faster classmates. Upon learning about Haiti's impossible victory over France in 1803 to liberate the island and blacks across the world, Pouchon is ready to use the motivation from Battaille de Vertiteres to fulfill his soccer dreams.
Children's Historical Fiction 978-1795490771

1803 SERIES WORKBOOKS (Student & Teacher's Editions)

The 1803 workbooks are designed to help young learners from K-12 practice the skills that are demanded of today's standards. Students will draw, write, create, and apply developmentally appropriate reading skills while using text-based evidence to answer questions.

ALSO BY BERWICK AUGUSTIN

NUMBERED WORDS
Words are powerful! They can either breathe or suffocate life. Many times wordiness can defeat the effectiveness of a message. This book is designed to convey succinct poems packed with powerful lessons. The poem's numerical number determines the amount of words it contains; the first one has 1 word while the fiftieth poem has 50 words.
Poetry/978-0999182208

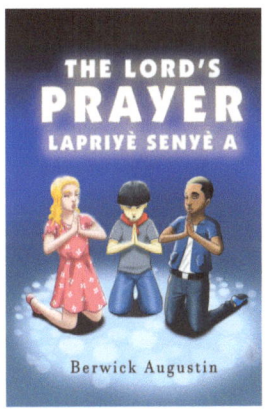

The Lord's Prayer
Berwick Augustin weaves his faith and culture into this bilingual book to creatively help parents teach their children the Lord's Prayer and the many lessons within it. In this book, you will find delightful illustrations, English and Haitian-Creole text, and discussion questions to empower all children to know that God created them just as they are.
Children Spiritual 978-1733076739

The Haitian-Creole Alphabet
In this book, Mr. Augustin simplifies the process of learning the Creole alphabets with colorful letters, illustrations, and the phonemic sounds.
This is a classic beginner's book that is perfect to teach children the Haitian ABCs or anyone else who is looking to build a foundation to learn the Haitian Creole language.
The book and coloring book are both available.
Children's Educational 978-1733076760

www.ingramcontent.com/pod-product-compliance
Lightning Source LLC
Chambersburg PA
CBHW050746110526
44590CB00003B/95